INTO Wild Thailand

BLACKBIRCH PRESS

An imprint of Thomson Gale, a part of The Thomson Corporation

THOMSON

GALE

Detroit • New York • San Francisco • San Diego • New Haven, Conn. • Waterville, Maine • London • Munich

© 2005 Thomson Gale, a part of The Thomson Corporation.

Thomson and Star Logo are trademarks and Gale and Blackbirch Press are registered trademarks used herein under license.

For more information, contact
Blackbirch Press
27500 Drake Rd.
Farmington Hills, MI 48331-3535
Or you can visit our Internet site at http://www.gale.com

Photo credits: cover, all pages © Discovery Communications, Inc. except for pages 7, 42 © Corel Corporation; pages 23, 35 © PhotoDisc

Discovery Communications, Discovery Communications logo, TLC (The Learning Channel), TLC (The Learning Channel) logo, Animal Planet, and the Animal Planet logo are trademarks of Discovery Communications Inc., used under license.

LIBRARY OF CONGRESS CATALOGING-IN-PUBLICATION DATA

Into wild Thailand / Marla Ryan, book editor.
 p. cm. — (The Jeff Corwin experience)
Includes bibliographical references and index.
ISBN 1-4103-0253-9 (hardback : alk. paper) — ISBN 1-4103-0254-7 (pbk. : alk. paper)
1. Animals—Thailand—Juvenile literature. 2. Wildlife conservation—Thailand—Juvenile literature. I. Ryan, Marla Felkins. II. Corwin, Jeff. III. Series.

QL317.I58 2004
591.9593—dc22   2004004488

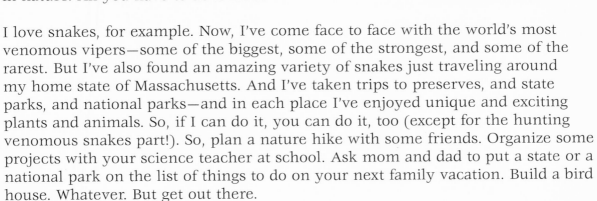

E ver since I was a kid, I dreamed about traveling around the world, visiting exotic places, and seeing all kinds of incredible animals. And now, guess what? That's exactly what I get to do!

Yes, I am incredibly lucky. But, you don't have to have your own television show on Animal Planet to go off and explore the natural world around you. I mean, I travel to Madagascar and the Amazon and all kinds of really cool places—but I don't need to go that far to see amazing wildlife up close. In fact, I can find thousands of incredible critters right here, in my own backyard—or in my neighbor's yard (he does get kind of upset when he finds me crawling around in the bushes, though). The point is, no matter where you are, there's fantastic stuff to see in nature. All you have to do is look.

I love snakes, for example. Now, I've come face to face with the world's most venomous vipers—some of the biggest, some of the strongest, and some of the rarest. But I've also found an amazing variety of snakes just traveling around my home state of Massachusetts. And I've taken trips to preserves, and state parks, and national parks—and in each place I've enjoyed unique and exciting plants and animals. So, if I can do it, you can do it, too (except for the hunting venomous snakes part!). So, plan a nature hike with some friends. Organize some projects with your science teacher at school. Ask mom and dad to put a state or a national park on the list of things to do on your next family vacation. Build a bird house. Whatever. But get out there.

As you read through these pages and look at the photos, you'll probably see how jazzed I get when I come face to face with beautiful animals. That's good. I want you to feel that excitement. And I want you to remember that—even if you don't have your own TV show—you can still experience the awesome beauty of nature almost anywhere you go—any day of the week. I only hope that I can help bring that awesome power and beauty a little closer to you. Enjoy!

Best Wishes!
Jeff

INTO
Wild Thailand

NORTH
AMERICA

EUROPE

ASIA

Pacific
Ocean

Atlantic
Ocean

AFRICA

SOUTH
AMERICA

Indian
Ocean

Pacific
Ocean

AUSTRALIA

Bangkok is a vibrant city of six million people. But take any road that leads into the countryside, and before long you'll find a jungle filled with surprises—lizards and snakes, bears, elephants, bats, and some very big cats. Join me as we encounter the fantastic creatures that make their homes in this country.

I'm Jeff Corwin.
Welcome to Thailand.

We're in a rice paddy, but there's more than rice thriving here in Thailand.

We'll see venomous snakes...

and turtles...

We are in a rice paddy about sixty miles outside of Bangkok. More than just rice is growing and surviving here. This is actually a home for lots of creatures. You can find snails and other invertebrates, turtles, and snakes—many snakes—in this man-made habitat. We just have to keep an eye out and do a little digging.

And, with a little digging, we'll find all kinds of other amazing creatures in this vibrant habitat.

7

I have to be very careful with the python down there.

He's squeezing the life out of me!

Underneath this blanket of water hyacinth is a very large reptile that I want to grab before it grabs me. I have to watch out for his head because this snake can deliver a very potent bite.

Got him. This is a reticulated python, the longest type of snake in the world. There are records of reticulated pythons reaching well over thirty feet in length. This individual is probably about ten feet long. And he's showing us how he defends himself and takes down his prey. He is a constrictor. He squeezes the breath and life out

of the creatures he's going to eat. The marks along his lip, which look like gashes, are heat-sensing devices—thermal receptor sites—that he uses to detect warm-blooded prey. He'll reach out and strike, grab onto the prey with his teeth, and then wrap around it and swallow it whole.

Check out its orange eyes.

You can see his wonderful tongue coming in and out. He uses that tongue to taste the air, chemically tracking prey. And here's something else that's gorgeous about these animals—he has orange eyes, as orange as pumpkins.

Tasting the air with its tongue.

My hand is turning purple, and as the snake pulls his body back he's giving me a nice shoulder separation. So perhaps this is a good time to let the reticulated python go and say thanks to this great reptile for providing our first wildlife experience here in Thailand.

Here come some Asian elephants.

Want a close-up?

We've come to Thailand because this region can provide us with some of the best wildlife encounters that Southeast Asia has to offer. But I'm not only hoping to discover unique animals and pristine ecosystems like this rain forest. I also want to get a better understanding of the very complex relationship that exists between the people of Thailand and the wildlife that they've been living with for thousands of years. Wildlife is still being exploited here. A lot of the habitat has been pushed to the point of disappearing. But there's a positive side. A lot of work is being done to help protect animals, and I'm hoping we'll see that.

One creature that best represents the complex relationship between human beings and wildlife is this mighty giant, the Asian elephant. And I'm hoping that this huge, intelligent creature will serve as a vehicle to move us through this exciting world.

Elephants are kind of hard to steer, though. It's like riding a boat. You want to go the right, you push to the left. You want to go to the left, you push to the right.

Humans and elephants share a unique relationship here.

Let's go inside, shall we?

Look at that! In that tree!

This is the Banglamung breeding center, located about two hours east of Bangkok. We want to move very quietly because we are in a very special place. It's a vast sanctuary that protects one of the rarest mammals in this part of the world, the Asiatic black bear.

An Asiatic black bear.

And look what's hanging in this tree—a huge black bear. He's staring right at me with that lionlike face, holding onto the tree with those daggerlike claws. Now, these are not tame bears. They tolerate human

presence; but they're not intimidated by us. They are predators, powerful carnivores. They have adapted to a great diversity of habitat, from tropical rain forest to snowy mountaintops.

See what he's doing? He's taking a great sniff, smelling something, perhaps us. Hopefully he's not thinking we're prey. If that is the case, I'm not worried because even though I can't outrun that bear, I sure can outrun you. Sorry. Survival of the fittest.

Check out those daggerlike claws.

These animals are solitary for most of their lives. They live about twenty-five years if they're lucky, foraging and exploring the wilderness. But males and females—boars and sows—come together to mate.

Smell something?

That was close. I thought I was going to be lunch.

He knows who's boss.

I wasn't sure what this bear was up to, so I moved out of his way and squatted down. Fortunately he just climbed a tree. Another great encounter—an Asiatic black bear showing us how he climbs the tree, walks on the ground, and makes the naturalist move away very quickly.

Not all the bears here are big enough to be dangerous. Look at this sweetheart. I am playing with an extraordinary animal, a Malayan sun bear. This individual is a four-month-old cub, a female.

Sun bears are the smallest species of bear in the world. They range from about 60 to about 120 pounds, maybe a little bit more for a very large individual. The bear gets its name from the golden crescent marking under its chin.

Goofing around with a Malayan sun bear.

Isn't she a sweetheart?

I wish you could hear the sound this bear is making—sort of "whoooo." That's a sound you find among all bears, from black bears to Malayan sun bears to polar bears. It's a sound of comfort, a sound that a young bear makes when interacting with its mother.

Careful. That's my ear.

I'm very happy to have had a chance to see this animal up close—even though she's acting fresh. Juvenile bears are just like human children. They're playful, and they're easily distracted.

Tag! You're it!

Lung Chung will lead us to the caves.

Our next destination is Sai Yok National Park. We're with Lung Chung, the leading village elder in this region. He's our guide to an intricate limestone cave system nestled deep in these hills. Getting there isn't easy, but Lung Chung, who's eighty-two, makes the trip every day. He is one of the only people who knows exactly where to find a very tiny creature that lives here.

This light's too bright. Time to switch to night vision.

Once we're deep inside the cave, we have to switch to night vision, so the bright lights don't scare these sensitive creatures away. I set up a mist net. I'm hoping to catch a bat inside this cave—a very special bat, an amazing bat. But while

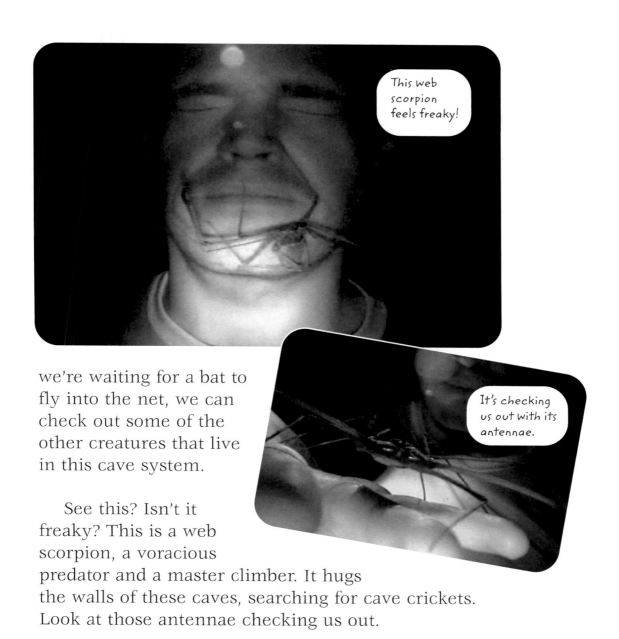

This web scorpion feels freaky!

It's checking us out with its antennae.

we're waiting for a bat to fly into the net, we can check out some of the other creatures that live in this cave system.

See this? Isn't it freaky? This is a web scorpion, a voracious predator and a master climber. It hugs the walls of these caves, searching for cave crickets. Look at those antennae checking us out.

I can't believe I netted one of these!

A Kitti's hog-nose bat.

Look at this— this is exactly what I wanted to find. I have just netted the smallest flying mammal on planet. I have to be so careful because this is a very fragile animal.

Isn't this cool? It is a Kitti's hog-nose bat. Its wingspan is only about four inches. Its body measures only a couple of inches from the tip of its nose to the tip of its tail, and it weighs only two and a half to three grams. It's a tiny, delicate creature, an animal you can find in only one place in the world, and that is Thailand.

This creature navigates through the night sky and finds its prey through echolocation. Like other bats, it produces high-frequency sound waves. Check out its ears—they are like satellite dishes. Those are the tools this animal uses to receive echoes of the sound that it screams out into the night sky. The echoes tell the bat what's ahead.

This bat is the smallest flying mammal in the world.

Those ears are the reason we had to set up a mist net to capture this bat. At first I was bouncing around in this cave like a drunken ballerina, trying to catch one. But these animals could hear me a mile away. Some scientists believe that they actually use sound waves to create an image of their environment. Through sound, the bat is almost seeing what he perceives as a potential predator—me.

Took me long enough to catch one.

What's in this hole?

A beautiful monocle cobra!

We're headed toward a little-known region of Thailand, really off the beaten path. But on the way, I can't resist exploring just one more rice paddy. You have to check this out—in this hole is a cobra. You can actually see the body and its scales. If I can catch it, we'll see what kind it is....

He's got some wicked fangs.

Look at this. Look at the hood on this guy. We have a beautiful monocle cobra. If you look inside this animal's mouth, you can actually see the fangs. The venom that this creature produces is a neurotoxin. That poison is designed to shut down the nervous system of its prey, literally turn the brain off, killing the prey.

Cobras are probably the most famous of the elapids, a group that includes other poisonous snakes such as kraits. The cobra has a very narrow head, but it spreads its hood when it's about to strike. Probably 99.9 percent of the time, it strikes when the hood is extended.

Got to hold him tight.

I'm holding this cobra firmly. I'm not hurting the snake, but I have to be very careful because there are lots of wonderful things I want to see in Thailand, and I don't want our adventure to end here in this rice paddy. I'm very glad we found this guy, because this is an animal I definitely wanted you to see.

When a cobra spreads its hood, it's ready to strike.

Ah. The moon is out.

Come out and play, nocturnal creatures!

It's night, my favorite time in the rain forest. The night here explodes with nocturnal creatures. Diurnal animals have gone to bed, and now the air is filled with a chorus of shrills, and squeaks, and chirps. Some creatures are out to eat, and some creatures are out to be eaten.

Wow, look at this—if I had moved quickly, I would have missed it. It's a beautiful white-lipped viper, just hanging in the tree branches. Isn't that great? I do not think I can capture him because he is about fifteen feet up.

Look at this white-lipped viper.

He's waaay up there.

You're going to love this, though. It's a gliding gecko. As the flying squirrels do back home, this lizard uses extra folds of skin, extra membranes, to create lift. When you look at it quickly, it looks like a regular gecko. But check this out—it has big webbed feet and extra flaps of skin along the sides of its body. The gecko goes to the end of a branch and leaps, and then spreads his legs and toes and glides to the next tree. What a wonderful creature.

Have you ever seen a gliding gecko?

Extra flaps of skin help him glide through the air.

See up in those branches?

Twined around a hanging branch I've found what I think is a whip snake or vine snake—a perfect rain-forest snake. You can tell he's in alarm mode. He sort of puffs up the front part of his body, spreading those green scales and exposing the white skin and the black scales below. That way, he looks a bit fierce, so you won't eat him. Up in the branches is where he likes to be, and that's where we're going to set him free.

This vine snake is the perfect rain forest snake.

What a great night this was. We found all sorts of fantastic creatures, and now what I really want to find is my pillow.

In southern Thailand, near Phuket Island, the Elephant Help Project is working hard to keep the remaining elephants in Thailand healthy. This nonprofit group supports the elephant population here by employing them in tourist activities, such as jungle rides, and providing free medical care to all the elephants in the

Phuket Island

Time to help the Elephant Help Project.

Dr. Eu knows all about elephants.

One needs a shot.

area. We're with Dr. Eu, a veterinarian who makes weekly visits to check up on local elephants. He has been working with elephants his entire professional life, basically all day every day, and much of that time is volunteer.

One has a splinter in its foot.

Dr. Eu shows us how to give an elephant a shot—in this case, an injection to help the elephant's metabolism. Then we check out an elephant that has a splinter between his toes. We hoist his foot up so we can work on it, get the splinter out, and then put on some antiseptic powder to cut down on infection.

And one's ... constipated?

In there?

Next, we've got an elephant that's constipated. If you're just sitting down to a meal, you may want to wait a while before picking up the fork. Dr. Eu has asked if I want to get involved with this, so here we go. And how does Jeff Corwin help an elephant? He reaches up the elephant's rectum and unblocks it. Whoo! My gosh, this elephant needs more fiber. Seriously, the diet of these elephants is not as diverse as it would be in the wild, so they tend to get constipated. But this one's OK now.

I feel something. Wish I didn't.

These three
youngsters are
a handful.

Their mahout isn't having much
luck teaching them manners.

The Help Project cares for young elephants as well. As you can see, I've got three adorable and extremely curious elephants hanging about me. Each one of these elephants is working with a mahout, a person who is a master at manipulating these animals. The job of the mahout is to train and teach his elephant to conduct itself properly and politely.

Elephants produce a whole range of sounds, not just the squeals and trumpets we're familiar with. The

trunk, especially the nasal area, is excellent for generating sounds. Some of the sounds are so deep that humans can't hear them. Here's something else that's interesting about the trunk. Look at the tip—it has a little digit. That single digit is unique to Asian elephants. An African elephant has what appear to be two digits.

She's showing off her trunk.

These guys are mugging me for peanuts. Asian elephants, very wonderful and very curious creatures.

Just one digit.

I'm all out of peanuts. Really.

The island
of Katong is
home to ...

This is the island of Katong. And if you look through the branches, you can see leaves shimmering and shaking. That usually means that somewhere, tucked behind the foliage, is a very rare and interesting primate called the gibbon. These animals look like monkeys, but in fact they are apes.

Gibbons!
They like to
hang out.

On the beach at Katong, I've spotted a solitary gibbon. These animals spend 99.9 percent of their lives up in the treetops, moving through the dense foliage of the forest canopy. But in the rare

moments when they're on the ground, they have the ability to go upright for short distances, sort of skipping along.

This fellow is waiting for food, and I'm keeping an eye on him. I've been warned about the gibbons on this island; they can be aggressive. There are people that have said, "Oh, look at the cute little gibbon." And the next thing they say is, "Get it off me, ma!"

Gibbons can even walk upright.

This loner is hoping some food will come along.

See why they're called white-handed gibbons?

Whoo whoo! That's a gibbon call.

This species is the white-handed gibbon. They come in two different color phases, the blonde and the chocolate. Like all gibbons, they're very vocal creatures. The bond between male and female or between offspring and parent is tightened with calls. If you're ever in the rain forest in the morning, you'll hear them calling—whoo, whoo, whoo. Each family unit has its own variation on that song.

In Thailand there is a big problem with people stealing animals from their natural environments.

You'll see people walking around with baby gibbons that have been taken from the wild. They do this so tourists can have a picture with a baby gibbon. And for a time, everybody loves the baby—he'll hang onto you and love you. But he's going to grow up and become dangerous and a nuisance. Then people don't want to deal with that gibbon anymore. If he's lucky, he ends up in a rehabilitation program, maybe on an island like this.

A mother gibbon and her baby share a strong bond, but some people steal baby gibbons from the wild.

Looks like a venomous viper.

It's time to head back to the mainland for more adventure in the rain forest.

I've just caught a very nice snake. It looks like a venomous viper. It has what seem to be thermal receptor sites, like a viper's. It has a triangular head, viperlike scales, even vertical eye pupils like a viper. But looks can be deceiving. This animal is a mock viper. It survives by mimicry, or imitation. Predators are fooled into thinking that it's poisonous, so they leave it alone.

But looks can be deceiving.

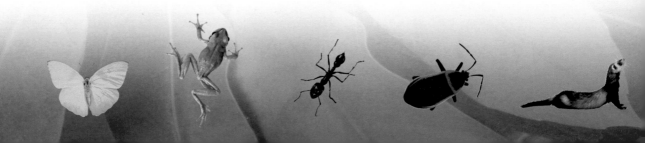

Its really a mock viper, and isn't venomous at all.

Ow! It bit me!

This snake not only looks just like a viper, it even behaves like one. When it feels threatened, it will coil up and bite. And now I am really hoping that, indeed, this is a mock viper, because it just bit me.

That just goes to show you...tough things come in little packages.

The snake taught me a good lesson. It's armed with some pretty sharp teeth that hurt when they nail you. It's not venomous, but it shows that tough things come in little packages, including these little mock vipers.

Darn it, buddy. I thought we were friends, and here you pull that stuff on me.

Welcome to my world. We're in Kanchanaburi Province, in a spooky, eerie swamp that is surrounded by a dense bamboo forest. That wall of bamboo has protected a creature that was unknown to scientists until 1983. It's a very unusual, brilliantly colored crustacean. To find it, you have to look inside the little casts and tunnels you see in the swamp.

It's kind of spooky in this swamp, but we're going to find a very unusual crustacean here.

Gotcha! I'll just clean off this Queen Sirikit's crab so we can see ...

Got one. Come here, you little crabby. Isn't it neat? It's called Queen Sirikit's crab. Because this species is so new to science, there is little I can tell you about it. It was named for a queen because of its very patriotic colors. The colors of Thailand are red, white, and blue. You can see that the crab's carapace (the top part of the shell) has sort of a bluish, purply hue. The sides of the carapace are white. And at the mouth, you can see red. Red, white, and blue—the patriotic crab.

Red, white, and blue. Now that's a patriotic crab!

I usually don't like cages...

but this one is very special.

This is the Kampangsaen Wildlife Sanctuary just west of Bangkok. We're inside an enclosure. Normally, I don't like to spend a lot of my time in a cage, but this is different. We're getting a chance to work one-on-one with one of the rarest and most beautiful felines here in Thailand.

Look at this beautiful face.

The clouded leopard is near extinction because hunters and traders crave its gorgeous fur.

This cat is called the clouded leopard because of the unique pattern of marbling you see across its coat. And it's the beauty of this animal's coat that makes it so rare. Fur traders have hunted it to near extinction.

This one might be pregnant.

This individual, a female, just might be pregnant. Her behavior has changed in the last week or so. If she is pregnant, that's great news. As far as I know, there has only been one other time when clouded leopards have successfully bred and produced offspring in captivity.

I hope she is. Don't you?

The clouded leopard—another example of the extraordinary creatures that have made a home here in Thailand. You know, part of me just wants to go over there and give her a nice back rub. But the other part of me likes to have fingers.

This cub is only four months old.

Check out his big feet.

Here is something I want you to see. It's a tiger, only about four months in age. He weighs about thirty pounds. Look in that mouth. One day those teeth will shear bone and muscle apart. Look at his coat. The brown tones will help him blend in with the earth and the bark, and the bars will break up his shape so his the prey can't see him. And look at those feet, look at the size of them. They're padded so that when he jumps, he's practically silent. Inside those paws are huge, very sharp claws. They're retracted, but when he's in hunt mode they'll come right out to dig into the hide of a samba deer or whatever this animal is hunting.

The conservation and protection of these big native cats is pursued here by a group of Buddhist monks. Chun, the abbot at this

monastery, is in charge of keeping order. This place is a sanctuary for wildlife of many kinds, but Chun's favorite is the tiger. And that's why we've come, to see some tigers in a very interesting situation.

Chun is in charge of this sanctuary.

There are about ten tigers in the sanctuary, and several of them are in this tiger pit. I've got my stick, but I'm getting a little nervous. These tigers have been freed from inhumane captivity or orphaned by poachers. They are unable to live in the wild, so they will spend the rest of their lives here at the monastery. See, they're just one big happy family here—except in this family, if you get a licking from your brother, you lose your arm.

Well, playtime is over, and it's time to head back to the main building, where the tigers sleep and are fed. The level of trust and respect paid to the tigers is always apparent here. While they may have shelter and

The monks take great care of these lucky tigers.

people to look after them, these tigers are still wild animals, and they are by no means domesticated.

We've seen some extraordinary creatures on our journey through Thailand. And this is a great way to end—with the most mighty creature of all, the beautiful tiger. I'll see you on our next adventure.

I'll see you on our next wild adventure!

Glossary

baht Thai currency

carapace the upper shell of a crab or similar animal

carnivores meat eaters

digit fingerlike projection

diurnal active during the day

diversity variety

echolocation a way of navigating by sending out and receiving sound waves

ecosystems communities of living things and the surroundings in which they live

environment the surroundings and conditions that affect living things and their ability to survive

habitat the place where a plant or animal naturally lives

mahout an elephant trainer

membranes thin bands of skin or other tissue

metabolism the process through which living things convert food into energy and living tissue

mimicry imitation

neurotoxin a poison that acts on the nervous system

nocturnal active at night

predators animals that kill and eat other animals

primate a member of a group of animals that includes monkeys, apes, and humans

venom poison produced by an animal

wingspan the distance from the tip of one outstretched wing to the tip of the other

Index